When I Say Ghost, I Don't Mean Dead

Zachary Kluckman

Winner of the Two Sylvias Press Chapbook Prize

Two Sylvias Press

Copyright © 2025 Zachary Kluckman

All rights reserved. No part of this book may be reproduced in any form without the written permission of the publisher, except for brief quotations embodied in critical articles and reviews.

Two Sylvias Press
PO Box 1524
Kingston, WA 98346
twosylviaspress@gmail.com

Cover Art: Sublimages
Cover Design: Kelli Russell Agodon
Book Design: Annette Spaulding-Convy
Author Photo: Andrew Torn
Contest Judge: Oliver de la Paz

Created with the belief that great writing is good for the world, Two Sylvias Press mixes modern technology, classic style, and literary intellect with an eco-friendly heart. We draw our inspiration from the poetic literary talent of Sylvia Plath and the editorial business sense of Sylvia Beach. We are an independent press dedicated to publishing the exceptional voices of writers.

For more information about Two Sylvias Press please visit:
www.twosylviaspress.com

First Edition. Created in the United States of America.

ISBN: 978-1-948767-25-5

Two Sylvias Press
www.twosylviaspress.com

Praise for *When I Say Ghost, I Don't Mean Dead*

"The lyric urgency gleams into the eye of the reader like the quick sunstruck reflection of light of a knife-blade. The shadows and the haunts that inhabit *When I Say Ghost, I Don't Mean Dead* startle and amaze. While the images of spiders alighting on a sleeper's face or the delicate rise and collapse of ribs in exhalation are a sign which may cause readers to flinch, there are other signs that resonate with beauty. This is an extraordinary meditation on the apparitions that keep pace with us, stride for stride."
~**Oliver de la Paz** (Contest Judge), author of *The Diaspora Sonnets* and *The Boy in the Labyrinth*

✤

"This is a striking, haunting collection on loss, alienation, the body, and the struggles of navigating familial and working-class trauma in the midst of societal expectation and scorn. Zachary Kluckman sings with tender ache, justified passion, alarming vision, and soul-stirring memory. A dynamic exhalating collection!"
~**Jose Hernandez Diaz**, author of *The Parachutist* and *Bad Mexican, Bad American*

✤

"The poems in *When I Say Ghost I Don't Mean Dead* dance at the boundary of what we can barely see. Kluckman writes: 'Life fits the body until it doesn't' in a collection imbued with vibrational energy. Brimming beyond our body-contours there are ghost-contours, realms of ecstatic light. Where do we meet our own edges, the parts of us most vulnerable to desire, to transformation? Do we hold our ghosts or do they hold us? The poems wrestle with these questions only to shatter them open, to resist any clear containment or delineation between the living and the dead. The dead whisper, yearn, break frenetically through our fractures. We are left wondering how to fold into the spaces left over. In the face of loss, all forms of touch–the touch of the lover, of the earth, contact with the self– become a kind of salvation: 'How like prayer it is to be received as you come.'"
~**Sara Daniele Rivera**, author of *The Blue Mimes* (Graywolf Press, 2024), winner of the 2023 Academy of American Poets First Book Award.

"Compelling, accessible, and remarkably honest, *When I Say Ghost, I Don't Mean Dead* is filled with stark, realistic poems that paint an intimate portrait of identity, interpersonal struggles, loss, family, and the ever-present need for empathy. In these vibrant poems of community and biography, Kluckman showcases a true talent for imbuing the smallest human details with authenticity and layered meanings. Each poem maps out the human heart in relation to that larger human heart we all share together, in all their internal conflicts, with precision and grace. Overflowing with vivid language, *When I Say Ghost, I Don't Mean Dead* is both intellectually stimulating and emotionally engaging, reminding us of the beautiful complexities of being human."
~John Sibley Williams, author of *As One Fire Consumes Another* (winner of the 2018 Orison Poetry Prize) and *Skin Memory* (winner of the 2018 Backwaters Poetry Prize)

Acknowledgements

The author wishes to thank the Editors and publications listed below, which gave some of the poems from this collection a first home, at times in an altered version.

"It Takes Patience to Love a Trauma Survivor", "Saltshaker", "Mouth Harp", "Seismic", "Not How You Imagined It" and "Sublime" all appear in *Subnivean* Issue 8, 2023 (Subnivean Award Finalists). My sincere gratitude to Soma Mei Sheng Frazier and the staff at *Subnivean* for nominating "It Takes Patience to Love a Trauma Survivor" for a Pushcart Prize.

"Snow Fall on Haunted House", appeared in the *Inflectionist Review*, Issue 17, January 2024

"Discovery of an Unmarked Grave Near the Beach" and "Scene from a Trailer in Northern New Mexico" appeared in *Black Fox Review*, Issue 24, Winter 2023

"We Are Gathered" appeared in the *Bookends Review*, August 2024

"When the Rain Asks if You Remember a Name" appeared in the *Blue Mountain Review*, Issue 28, May 2023

"My Mother Reading Obituaries" appeared in *Crab Creek Review* 2023

I would also like to thank the following people, whose support and kindness have been a constant source of motivation and proof of the good that exists in the world on the hardest days. Thank you to Katrina Kaye and Rene Mullen for being willing readers of these poems as they were in development. Thank you to the New Mexico State Poetry Society, MindWell Poetry and all of the poets who are all a source of inspiration and uplift during the low tide moments. Thank you to Marcial and Stephanie Delgado for Voices of the Barrio and for your friendship. Thank you to Kristin Patton for reminding me why hugs are so important. Thank you to Serena Rodriguez, Savannah Rodriguez, Scarlett Cortez, JoAnna

Atencio and all of the kind spirits who remind me that it is possible to be possessed of joy as well. Thank you to everyone who has supported my wild, and at times reckless, pursuit of this art that keeps me alive. We have had some adventures! Deepest thanks to my children and grandchildren who every day remind me of the most important role I have in this world, providing a home and a safe space where love is the rule—for you and everyone who needs one. Thank you to *Albuquerque The Magazine* for naming me the 2024 Best Local Poet in a community so full of talent. My deep gratitude to JeanAnn Verlee and John Sibley Williams for your time and energy proofreading these poems and offering guidance. Also, my gratitude to Sara Daniele Rivera and Jose Hernandez Diaz for being early readers and providing such moving comments. Thank you sincerely to Oliver de la Paz for finding beauty in these poems and selecting this collection for the Two Sylvias Chapbook Prize and of course, thank you endlessly to Two Sylvias for providing such an enthusiastic and welcoming home for this work of several years. Thank you, reader, for picking up this collection and walking through this world and its multitude of hauntings with me. Remember, your existence matters. I am so glad you are here.

Table of Contents

roughstock   / 1
    when i say
It Takes Patience to Love a Trauma Survivor   / 4
Mouth Harp   / 6
When I Say Ghost, I Don't Mean Dead   / 7
Possession   / 8
Ghost Hunt on the Abandoned Farm   / 10
Saltshaker   / 12
Seismic   / 14
Haunting as Touch   / 15
Make Up Sex   / 17
Snow Fall on Haunted House   / 19
Not How You Imagined it   / 20
Haunting as Raked Leaves   / 22
    i don't mean
We Are Gathered   / 24
Ride On Horizon   / 25
Discovering an Unmarked Grave Near the Beach   / 27
Scene From a Trailer in Northern New Mexico   / 29
Ekphrastic: Mug Shot   / 31
My Mother Reading Obituaries   / 32
Independence Day   / 33
Every Story Eventually Writes Itself Out of an Author   / 35

When the Rain Asks If You Remember a Name   / 36

A Flock of Birds Falls from the Sky Without Explanation   / 38

About the Author   / 41

roughstock

you splash in arroyos behind
the corn with crawdads
the soles of your feet torn
with broken glass all
the beer bottles
discarded by your old man
no surprise his hurt can reach you here
absence no guarantee of safety
his anger winged like brittle bats
bottles explode against the walls
cigarettes like fireworks in your hair
you wash yourself clean with mud
softer than his hands dress
again with leaving adorn
yourself with absence trees
reaching every direction strangled
like silent films of summer storms
rain choking the irrigation
channels behind you all the ghosts
this town has known staring
from the tall grass as you plant
footprints in galloping strides
down the red clay you have never
been more horse than you are now wild
wind-blown hair swimming
behind you like a swarm of bees
children hang from monkey bars watch
you run who wants out
you who taunts their own shadow
every light in the mirror now
every window facing out there is
no parade when you escape

come this far and the horizon
knife blade brilliance
fills your smile with bloody freedom
bloody mouth but the last
pant as your legs pump okay
it's okay you will make it you
must the sound of a truck behind
you thunder-promise you
don't stop don't shake run
the city full of ancient gods
and curses no one will find you
there know you there
no one

when i say

It Takes Patience to Love a Trauma Survivor

The first gentle touch;

even this, like a dying rabbit's
tremor folds me into plow shapes. Furrowing the
sheets with my desperate hands. Escape

the shadow figures of memory who stand in rows
like evergreen tendrils climbing the walls.
It's not you, it's me. It's them.

How to explain the serpent intentions that bind me.
How they topple the headstones, set fire to the rows
of grapes. Stain me with their effluence. Their milk

clear and wet upon my lips. Even this sustaining blood
leaves my tongue dry. Be patient. Yours is the hand
that unlocks the basement door, that lights

the space between the seatbacks and the dresser.
Yours is the face in the window that signals escape.
Yours, the lighthouse in the backyard where I keep

two eggs and a map of the sky to tempt myself
into believing the stars can actually predict our movements.
Can direct me across the load-bearing sea of sheets

into your arms. Help me conjure this
sickle of night, this horizon of spun stars.
Bend me into constellations. Name the birds that rise

from my throat. Till the earth with my bent back.
The rain will recognize me then

as offering. As sacrifice. Your hands
will catch holy fire. The fields

will blaze with the shape of us. It will be worth
the time it took for us to arrive here.

The harvest at the end of a season of waiting.
The stars screaming with life.

Mouth Harp

You smell like you met rain in a dark alley
and it soured your cologne. Kissed you with
its milk breath and left you allergic. Fourteen
hours of weeping later you meet a man
in your mirror and ask him his name.
It's not uncommon to question yourself,
but you're wearing the same shirt you wore
the day you met your wife. Hard not to
recognize the hope tornado forming under
your umbrella. I've seen this before.
Someone made you think it's possible to love
popcorn without risking heart attack again.
Someone buttered you up with promises
like flower petals dripping from their sticky
fingers. I gotta hand it to you. Your ability
to believe in regular people makes you
seem almost superhuman. Almost mythical.
In school you took so many fists to the face
you returned your bruises for a nickel
per pound, your flesh felt priceless. Still
you did not find the value others see in you.
But hope, yes. Love, yes. Believe
in spirits with thread counts like Egyptian linen.
Believe it is possible to touch something
that returns it to you touch for touch.
The street performer on the corner
plays Stravinsky on the harmonica. Maybe
anything *is* possible.

When I Say Ghost, I Don't Mean Dead

I mean shadows make poor companions. The quiet
like a bird's eye. Every movement a dull impression.
What should elicit laughter ballooning away into
sunsets. Still, the magnolias are heavy with beauty
as if burdened.

A child sits on a park bench as if wrought of similar
iron. Mascaraed eyes or carefully drawn hieroglyphs.
Something ancient about him suggests a knowledge
of death. The merry-go-round spins its throatless song
into the grey.

I mean, he and I, there. Each awake to the sky. Blue
and blue and blue. Under the trees nearby a homeless
man stares at a photo and his beard grows longer.
Time is a eunuch abandoning its children. No wonder
we so often question

creation. I mean sit long enough with absence
you touch without touching ghost.

Possession

The neighbors report seeing a faceless figure sit doll-like
In my window at night. Listen, I won't feign surprise.

Sometimes I forget to wear my eyes. I paint them
On so carefully this dry erase expression mimics birds in flight.

My eyelashes grow in rows like shark teeth. Of course
I look startled. Waking each day surprises me; the way tigers

Arrive at the feast without their feet. Stealth and camouflage
Are defense mechanisms of superior beasts. When I hide

In the grass, someone always complains. I once believed
I had this chameleon DNA, but it was just youth trying again

To make sense of fear. I do not belong to some genus
Or species named in a Romantic tongue; am not that rare

Cryptid who emerges from the brush one sunny day
Surprised by the commotion I have caused. Just a man

Sopping wet with potential, as all good clay should be.
They say we are made in another's image and I wonder

If they mean frightened. If they mean so unsure of creation
A part of them is given nightly to wandering naked down

The halls, looking in doors as if unfamiliar with
The particular arrangement of rooms. Rooms full

Of butterflies battering the walls in their cavernous home.
A domed roof gives the illusion of freedom to the cage. My head

Works under a similar design. The random whorls of knot
In wood often lead me to question whose fingerprints these are.

In the feverish dark, don't we all hurl ourselves at shadows,
Looking for comfort in whatever shapes we can touch?

You are right not to question me when I speak of animals
In my flesh. A man so familiar with watching the ghosts

Erase themselves from mirrors is not to be trusted.
Hopeless romantic that he becomes, his mind is sure

To turn its hauntings outward. Someone should inform
The neighbors all of their houses are haunted. I have seen them

There in the windows, holding court with cold shadows.
Every room full of longing. Every memory a poltergeist.

Ghost Hunt on the Abandoned Farm

The well water holds three moons tonight.
Restless as the years since I've been back.
We stand near piñons comparing the sky
we'd like to see with the one currently
baring its teeth.

Wonder when stars fall if they plan
their route, or simply seek an escape.
If orbital planes grieve those who return
to the heavy bodies they thought
long behind them.

Winter scarecrows bob their heads
to a wind named shatter. Frost biting through straw.
Even the birds take pity for the night.
In absence, home feels more like home.
Familiar spirits

spinning through fields horizon
to hill. Where children learned to swim
in the well for salvation. Crawdads
for dinner over cold conversation.
Ice stitched

in the swollen wood of its frame,
this old house remembers harvest more
as prayer than religion. Blood
sacrificed to fear. The old man
whose hands'

scarred legacy creaks the door.
Footsteps heavy as memory on an empty
stair. A flurry of snow phantoms the yard.
In the shadow of hills smaller than
recalled, coyotes

drawn by our whispers, sneak out of view.
The trees kaleidoscope constellations.
Dimming with distance, dirt roads erase.
Under trees, dark bodies gather.
Soon, the storm

will come and wind will shriek
this house apart. The silence prepares
to sacrifice itself. We will lose nothing.

Saltshaker

Your head is a room full of people we barely know.
I entertain them with my storm clouds and fireworks

While we feast in bakeries near the graveyard. Who doesn't
Want their croissants to smell of newly-turned earth?

What kindness I have shown your tender ego. Frail kite
Waiting for another wind to lift you, spiraling, into heaven.

Pretending you are growing tall, I hunched my shoulders
So you can tell your friends how love made you

The girl who saved the urchin. The poor boy from the streets.
Who cut the roses and his toenails with the same scissors

In the effort to cultivate a more attractive yard.
You wouldn't want the neighbors to see how he

Dressed your ghost for bed each night. How he loved

You back to earth, every touch a séance. Don't
Tell you have forgotten how I washed you

When the windows exploded with the cold
The night you crawled into my room looking for someone

To save. When a thrift store mirror etched with fool's gold
Fell, you stared at me as if naming the animals.

I performed my first impression of cumulonimbus dynamism.
I thundered for you. Painted the sky with water and hung

Ties from every cloud. I dressed the weather for this party,
Then you uninvited me. The introvert inside of me usually leaves

Early anyway. But first, your favorite party trick. Pour a little
More salt in the wounds so they taste like you when I lick them.

Seismic

The spider crawls across my body while you sleep.
Her touch is lighter than yours. Lightning rattles the window
and I shudder with a random urge to push my tongue
against it like a loose tooth. The things we are soon
to lose ache like this. I remind myself I cannot

tie a string around your wrist and slam the door.
Your leaving will not bloody my mouth this time.
The kids will not expect a dollar under their pillows. Unless
they do. I cannot empty my wallet and fold your absence
inside. So I fold myself into origami smallness. Tight

with potential. Touch me and I will jump across
the room. Like this spider. She is more afraid of you than
you are of her they tell me. Funny, the assumptions
we make based on bodies. As if gender implies strength.
Or fear. What color is lightning? Blood

we recognize but not the light that splits the sky.
Not the hand that parts the sheets. The hand that moves
against my spine, strangles my crotch. Tell me
again how a tree falls in the forest without a sound.
I can promise you this. There is a sound

the dying make. As small as rain, every inch
of the falling is a note on the tectonic scale.
Earthquakes produce an eerie music, not unlike
the ghosts watching from the corner. All
the music available to us in this world

and here we are again, listening for a door.

Haunting as Touch

In darkness; depth unspeakable.

      Limits of perception erase the familiar.
      The ear becomes
           a lonely sailor seeking
           a cry across boundless seas.
      Raging waters have lost their tongue.

Distance means nothing to the stars.

A door closes under unseen hands.
Phantom palms measuring your surprise,

the jump is instinct.
      Less fear than
flesh reaching for a pinnacle.
Testing its escape.
Evidence you sought and found.
Evidence that light prevails, but absent
      suddenly your haunting carries meaning.

Whose fingerprints excite this flesh,
part your lips?
Only you
      and the unseen shape of other.
Do you fear possession? Or long
for capture, a touch
      as soft as invisible?

The soft hairs along your arm
rise in columns,
      near invisible fuzz
adoring your breasts.

Light never becomes unbearable.
Shapes of want.
      Breath does not escape
but leaves you.

Whatever ghosts you've come
to calm or claim, soon, those doors
      locked before you clamor to the floor.

Anyone might walk in on you
any second.
      Find your flesh, like this;
ripe with its desires.

Make Up Sex

      and if this house is a monster's ballroom,
then together we practice the mosh pit's magic. Storm

naked as weather through and under rafters,
setting fire to our sheets. Shadow puppets of touch

lift their heads from our skin. The windows fill
with ghost light. Your eyes are such terrible fire, everywhere

my hands settle, temples tremble. The dead
raise their hands to the moon even as the sun is setting

its cold feet between our thighs. We shudder
together like moths discovering fire. Something in this

requires us to love. Your fingernails, clean as syntax.
This wet place between us. Our hands reach across such incredible

distances we are almost close. I offer you rain
from the coffee can you keep under your windows. The sky

delivers us fever and we kiss as if the bitten tongue
sets caged animals free. If it's forgiveness you want, you are free

to leave. Or stay. Shapeshift in the mirror
until light takes our shadows for lovers. Slip last year's skin

from your shoulders. Each movement an exposure.
Bodies posed like trees in a photo of the solar eclipse, limbs

seeking a wet salvation. What is the tongue
but a root? What is a root but bondage to one body? Love

me or love me not. Whatever. The music
swells and our hands remember a kindness. A pleasure

we took once and more than once
under different skies. If it's freedom you want

turn the music up on your way.

Snow Fall on Haunted House

The image blurs. A television screen
seeking a signal. The old house with its gabled
roof collapsing. Ribs falling into a sigh of relief.
Hard to let go sometimes. The wooden doors hand
-carved. Nothing that lived
here ever knew a gentle touch. The old man
still searches for his bottle within. The bottle falling
from his hands became a shattered prism. Caught the firelight
as it flew into dark corners. The way he fell beside it. How his feet
lost their way in the wet. How he found the bottleneck
opening an exit he could not refuse. As you
could not refuse when your door admitted him.
How the shadows turned their heads.
The drink
always in his gut, the spirits called him home
that night. What would he do
if he found his last drink now. Remember,
a small voice whispers behind the curtain of lungs
where you have been held captive by his memory.
Remember what happened when he found
you. A palpable absence in the frigid
air. Steam escaping our lungs as we listen
to the silence growing around us.

Not How You Imagined it

Wind crosses the boneyard, oil and rust
brought to your nose. The chickens lay eggs in hubcaps.
Prying quarters from gumball machines
someone forgot to empty, by now a memory.
Your feet too big for catholic school. Faith
like spiders under the nails. You itch
with adolescence, race motorcycles
in the rain. Anything to escape.
Crawl inside of lovers with your fingers,
scratching cobwebs from your palms.

Your body is learning.
How the wind makes kite tails of your hair.
Fills your nose with salt seas far from here.
Your shirt billows with invisible winds. Draw
lighthouses on your arms, burn candles
on parchment and perfect your signature.
Hard times seem simpler. Dark ages
pressed between the pages of your books.
Adventure. Love. The romance you imagine
caught like torn linen in the trees.

You used your hands once to blacken the eyes
of a boy who called you chicken. Youth
remembered as junkyard. As charnel house.
As ten-foot fences. Enter
adulthood as refugee. Life raft built
with the bones you have broken. The teeth
lost in heater grates. The chickens
screaming in the yard as the wolf settles
its weight against their door. How the feed
rattles from their bowls.

You dream of rust and ghosts with eyes
like headlights. Bury seeds from every tree
that blooms. A future full of hiding places planted.
Wash your hands, the thin leather skin
becomes with time. Dye your hair a color
you remember from a dream of the sea.
Adjust your crown of flowers
as you settle into your chair. Somewhere
a woman you once loved
moves your photograph to a shoebox.

Haunting as Raked Leaves

leaves swirl like dizzy ghosts   unsettled settlers in this autumnal land
what must it be like to return to the place escape was promised
i understand it is only the wind that stirs them   a brief zephyr reminding
us that fall has many meanings   what is it about the cold that feels
like gathering   are we prepared   when the snows come will we huddle
with animals like our ancestors   domestication only another word
meaning lonely   like marriage   every love

is a long-distance relationship   until your ghosts have forgiven you i don't mean

We Are Gathered

The faces behind the trees wither
in the radiance of will-o'-the-wisps.
My granddaughter before she is born.
To the uninitiated eye this blood
as thin as moonlight ribbons loss.
For those who have lost more than life
there are rivers deeper than oceans
ascending these hills and hollows.
Bone is a dull bell the winter rings
into shapes of haunting, melodies
that compose your specific gravity.
Returning limb for limb the weight
of absent children. The pregnant womb
emptied by the callous moon. Eyes
of bloodshot destiny, hands made to cradle
the flower of youth that will never bloom.
The earth turns away from such use.

Tell me, am I wrong to pull
the dead into conversation, seeking the name
she would have carried among
their number? Did she open my daughter's
heart only to crawl inside and lie
inside her, moss gathering a gentle rain?
Kneeling now beside a silence multiplied,
their eyes closed to heaven,
I beg the quiet to remember
what stars they might have carried.

Ride On Horizon

Inspired by "Constellation Route" by Matthew Olzmann

…and what if that one rider
on horseback, lonely beneath the stars
rides on to the end as you say
    and continues

        on into the stars; into
        the inevitable consequence
        of loss. Of getting lost. What if

he becomes

        the constellation another soul endeavors
    to decipher while seeking its own direction.

Aren't these amnesiac shapes
we assign our own forgotten names to
a kind of hieroglyph?
    A way of mapping

        our movements
        through the incalculable

distances. Even now two

people stand only feet apart
staring at the very same star. Sextant eyes
plotting a course. Separate
    journeys

                    to unfamiliar homes.
                    Last night we witnessed
                    our youngest child

erase the moon scars
from his arms with a single decision.
I wonder at the ease with which we lose
ourselves in the smallest spaces.
          How small a home

                              becomes in the distance.
                              A moment sometimes
                    all the time required

to forget your place on earth.

Discovering an Unmarked Grave Near the Beach

After listening for ocean, we turn the skull
on its side and move to avoid the runaway water.

This is how I assume drowning sounds,
a swell of tides so choral you can no longer

tell the moon's influence from the pulse
of your own heart beating. They say there is a simple

music to surrender, to letting go of everything
once loved. Forgetting the shape of your own foot,

the countless steps taken to prove yourself
among the living. In school we were taught addition,

made to believe we could be more than
residents in these bodies, more than history's witnesses.

What have we learned, grandfather? Mother,
don't we wear the same pride on our faces when

slinging arrows across fences? Don't we
still attempt to kill our neighbors because their flowers

would look better in our graveyards? Water them,
then. Let us fill these vessels with fluid, these bodies

with their life-giving sweetness, their holy water.
Let us pour our lives into this ground as if oceans

did not whisper close by, and pat ourselves
on the back with these dirty hands. These dirty

bloody hands, hands like shovels digging
grave after grave. I tell you, if you hold another

animal's skull close to your own,
you can still hear their mothers weeping.

Scene From a Trailer in Northern New Mexico

They found her because the dog was hungry.

His ribs began to show
        laying day after day on the porch.

Eventually their concern for the dog
led her neighbor to call someone. Bring the police.
Your mother, two months gone, lay next to
her pills. Not suicide, they assure you.

Proof she was finally getting some help.

Two months alone on her floor. Heart
destroyed by smoke. Maybe the cigarettes.
Maybe the lack of phone calls. Maybe she needed
a hug. Bent over her hurt, you picture her

stretching for the phone, wonder whose name
she called out. Yours or your sister's.

If either. Or if she was so alone with her fear
even the names would not come.

Imagine your grief is a button, a friend says,
inside of a box someone has dropped a ball
inside. At first it ricochets off the walls so fast
the button is constantly pressed. Over time

the ball will bounce with less force, press
your button less often until it stops.

You say, imagine grief was my mother's heart.
That's what the pills were for.

You say, they found her
because the dog was hungry.

You say
no one knew for two months.

You say —

Ekphrastic: Mug Shot

A daughter straightens the wilted flowers in a field knowing
she cannot invent a strength for them. These long stalks will
fall among the buzzing dead. Horse flies and bees compete
for first chair in this symphony of winged instruments.
Like stones thrown between the trees her name echoes
from a distance. An unfamiliar voice, insistent. Every cloud
takes up the shape of centipedes, given to their eternal crawl
through heather. Every blackened eye she has worn rises
in her mind like the blood moon. A fever flush aloe cannot
soothe. The daughter thinks of her father's arms; a safety
she cannot reach so far from home. How many times
has he saved her? Tried to save her. Her hands welcome
the drying sun. Drop the whetted blade that opened her
lover's hunger, fed him a medicine of his own concoction.
Red and blue, the lights swirl as simple as gravity, through
the trees. Approaching fast as she pulls and pulls the grass
from the earth's face. Just once to see the world laid bare
before her. Just once to touch the world without fear.

My Mother Reading Obituaries

As if she does not know. As if she is not there
even now, occupying both worlds. Her body
a lock through which she exits and returns. Shade

on the linoleum. Purple halo on the wall when
the sun tilts its head in witness. Umbrella
of crows opening over power lines. Or the hawk

chasing them. More like her; to be the biggest
voice in the crowd. To interrupt a murder with her
wings cocked. Sharp eyes bright as pistols in

the glass display. Remember how she took you
to all those thrift stores seeking gods. Garage sales.
How you carried home boxes of books. Devoured

stories character by storied character. The pages
blurring as you read. How she would listen as you
described them. Rocking back and forth on her

bed, legs crossed. Listening to you perhaps.
Or half, to a sound beyond the edge of reason.
Someone calling her bodily into the tesseract.

A word you carried from a wrinkle in time.
A fold in the page constricting space/time. Holy,
Holy! Travel between worlds made possible

on the backs of words. On the pale blue lips
of that great whale swimming towards you. Through
the earth. The universe opening its single eye

inside that impossible maw.

Independence Day

Metal drums, plastic bins, electric tangerine spray
painted names; the walls are bored with dressing
the same new age defiance colors.

Flags and gang tags. Everyone so focused on
what color you wear around here, the conversation
stays only skin-deep. Before the streetlights flicker out

with their nightly impatience,
a young boy will die.

We will run our fingers down the newsprint
seeking familiarity. Seeking names that call out
asking if I have written one about them yet.

An elegy or a eulogy, the only difference;
how we dress things up for the occasion.

Birds eat whatever worm the earth turns up.
The earth feasts with the same indifference. Early
or not a meal is a meal. But we, with our

sweet suede couches and gas-powered barbeques,
don't we smell of burning? Pale white ghosts cooking
pork chops as the neighbor kid runs past.

Cops with blued steel phalluses rising from
their meaty thighs, barrels bruising the darkness
with their bark. Someone in the yard asks who

was it this time? Another body colored like peel away
targets at the firing range. Another cop going on vacation.
It's not just veterans who cringe when

the fireworks go off. Down the street, a woman wearing
her favorite nightgown will cling to her son's body,
blood staining the white fabric under blue

skies. Such clear blue skies.

You could almost believe,
freedom was more than just a little
white lie.

Every Story Eventually Writes Itself Out of an Author

His pale skin there in the window
lessening, heavy-bodied with moon.
Practicing his ghost pose.
The way he'll stand for all eternity in a corner
catching cold.
Cancer in his eyes. Cancer in his throat. Cancer consuming
the flowers in his garden.
Pale butterflies, devoid of color; homeless in the darkening.
A book falls, flat as life's ending.
I always turn to the last page first because I want to know
how it all ends, he said once.
If I'd said what I meant to then—that any point in the story
can serve as conclusion, some
open-ended as questions, some chosen
because the protagonist has found his meaning
in whatever
accident of love life delivers—if I'd told him
how often the author is themselves
a bystander, he might have risen
from his bed, bandages falling from his skin like mosquitos
to look once more out
across the parking lot, watch the unhoused couple
with their shopping cart
form a tent of canvas beneath the neon cross.
All I ever wanted was a river. A grass as soft as winter.
To lie in the sun and write.
I'm consumed with guilt for creating them.
For burdening my characters with this impossible goal.

Imagine
asking them
to survive their own creation.

When the Rain Asks If You Remember a Name

There is only your response, only your milk-empty voice
in a barren room. Only the remembered flicker of flames
long dead where no one has tended the fire. Your vision
is a grey fade of ash under rain. How long it has been since
you understood your own body, since the absence of callous
from your hands. How long since the full light reached
your eyes, unbetrayed.

The weakening edges of once plain sight blur the past.
Remember all the holes you dug with your best friend,
a name half-forgotten, in the yard. How the cavernous
walls trembled with thunder when the storm came.
How it felt under your hands, pressed to the walls
of those holes. What it taught you of hearts; those
engines of spring.

Your breath holds a secret you are still trying to learn.
Your pulse then and now a conductor, booking
passage while ticking its counter. The veins in your hands
a train track to the past and back. The journey not
what you planned, but all your time underground is
the reason your voice caught an echo. Even now
in your kitchen, making plans

by matchlight with the ghosts of color and fall
for your next endeavor within the earth's hunger,
your mother calls from the past. Whispers remember
how she always said life is not a pile of leaves
you gather in the yard, but the bronze sail of autumn.
The falling and everything that happens on the way.
Your body is not a temple

but the door that welcomes the faithful.
How like prayer it is to be received as you come.
To raise your eyes from the trees as the forgotten
name returns and smile as the shovel completes
its ritual.

A Flock of Birds Falls from the Sky Without Explanation

Avian distress. Twenty-six bodies on the ground of unknown cause.
Of unreal physics. Flight interrupted by the sudden limit.
Life fits the body until it doesn't. With its too-sweet appetites
plucked from trees, its mouth full of gravel. The worm emerges
with no consideration. Hunger has its own set of ethics. Once
in a town not unlike this, a flock of birds plummeted as if agreed.
Species. Color. Irrelevant to the worm. A gift of whatever gods
the earthbound speak of beneath the mantle. Another, different time,
my mother gathered seven plaster buddhas painted gold and a single feather.
Took up religion with no name. *What matter,* she said, *how we call
towards heaven.* The sky can only hold so many voices. *You'd be lucky
to be heard.* I imagine her now, reading of this small extinction. Some say super
-natural evidence, bloodless and feathered. Others flagellate
themselves in a frenzy of *forgive me fathers*. My mother, whose faith
was a revolving door, would only nod, as if all of this
only confirms her suspicions.

Your first mistake, of course, is thinking the dead silent.
    You cannot contain what contains you.

Zachary Kluckman is a nationally ranked slam poet with work in print worldwide, including *New York Quarterly, New Writing Scotland, Cutthroat, Crab Creek Review, Arts & Letters, Cagibi, the Pedestal* and *Blue Mountain Review*. A multi-award-winning writer and spoken word artist, Kluckman was a Finalist for the 2023 Subnivean Poetry Awards judged by Kazim Ali and received Honorable Mention as a Finalist for the 2024 Jack McCarthy Poetry Prize. Kluckman won the Red Mountain Press National Poetry Prize in 2012 and a Gold Medal from the Scholastic Arts & Writing Awards. He is the author of three previous poetry collections; *The Animals in Our Flesh* (Red Mountain Press, 2012), *Some of It is Muscle* (Swimming with Elephants Publications, LLC, 2013) and *Rearview Funhouse* (Eyewear Publishing, 2023). His new collection, *When I Say Ghost, I Don't Mean Dead* was selected by Oliver de la Paz as the winner of the Two Sylvia's Chapbook Prize.

Winners of the Two Sylvias Press Chapbook Prize

2024 — *When I Say Ghost, I Don't Mean Dead* by Zachary Kluckman
   Judge: Oliver de la Paz

2023 — *Letters, Unwritten* by Andrew Robin
   Judge: Eduardo C. Corral

2022 — *The Call of Paradise* by Majda Gama
   Judge: Diane Seuss

2021 — *At Night My Body Waits* by Saúl Hernández
   Judge: Victoria Chang

2020 — *Hallucinating a Homestead* by Meg Griffitts
   Judge: Traci Brimhall

2019 — *Deathbed Sext* by Christopher Salerno
   Judge: Maggie Smith

2018 — *American Zero* by Stella Wong
   Judge: Danez Smith

2017 — *In the House of My Father* by Hiwot Adilow
   Judge: Kaveh Akbar

2016 — *Arab in Newsland* by Lena Khalaf Tuffaha
   Judge: January Gill O'Neil

2015 — *Naming the No-Name Woman* by Jasmine An
   Judge: Keetje Kuipers

2014 — *Earth* by Cecilia Woloch
   Judge: Aimee Nezhukumatathil

www.ingramcontent.com/pod-product-compliance
Lightning Source LLC
Chambersburg PA
CBHW051703040426
42446CB00009B/1287